MAY 0 7 2007

World of Reptiles

Horned Lizards

by Jason Glaser

Consultants:
The Staff of Reptile Gardens
Rapid City, South Dakota

Capstone
press

Mankato, Minnesota

Bridgestone Books are published by Capstone Press,
151 Good Counsel Drive, P.O. Box 669, Mankato, Minnesota 56002.
www.capstonepress.com

Library of Congress Cataloging-in-Publication Data
Glaser, Jason.
    Horned lizards / by Jason Glaser.
      p. cm.—(Bridgestone books. World of reptiles)
    Includes bibliographical references and index.
    ISBN-13: 978-0-7368-5421-4 (hardcover)
    ISBN-10: 0-7368-5421-5 (hardcover)
    1. Horned toads—Juvenile literature. I. Title. II. Series.
QL666.L267G55 2006
597.95'4—dc22
                                      2005022531

Summary: A brief introduction to horned lizards, discussing their characteristics, range, habitat,
    food, offspring, and dangers. Includes a range map, life cycle diagram, and amazing facts.

Editorial Credits
Megan Schoeneberger, editor; Enoch Peterson, set designer; Kim Brown and Patrick Dentinger, book
    designers; Jo Miller, photo researcher; Scott Thoms, photo editor; Tami Collins, illustrator; Nancy
    Steers, map illustrator

Photo Credits
AnimalsAnimals/Raymond Mendez, 20
Corbis/David A. Northcott, 4
Lynn M. Stone, 6
Root Resources/Anthony Mercieca, cover
Visuals Unlimited/Joe McDonald, 1, 10
W.C. Sherbrooke, 12, 16, 18

1 2 3 4 5 6 11 10 09 08 07 06

Table of Contents

4

Horned Lizards

If you saw a horned lizard, you might think you were looking at a toad. Like toads, horned lizards have wide, flat bodies. In fact, horned lizards are often called "horny toads." But they are not toads at all.

Horned lizards are reptiles. Reptiles are **cold-blooded** animals and need outside heat to keep warm. Like other reptiles, horned lizards have scaly skin and grow from eggs.

◄ Horned lizards have large mouths and wide bodies. The scientific name for horned lizards, *Phrynosoma*, means "toad bodied."

What Horned Lizards Look Like

Horned lizards look like pocket-size dinosaurs. Adults measure only about 5 inches (13 centimeters). Horned lizards have horns that crown their heads. Some horned lizards also have pointed spines along their sides. Hungry animals often choose to stay away from a lizard's sharp spines and horns.

Horned lizard skin has a mix of colors. To hide from **predators**, horned lizards blend in with the world around them. Their skin has shades of yellow, brown, tan, and black.

◀ The colors on the horned lizard's body blend in with rocks and dead leaves.

Horned Lizard Range Map

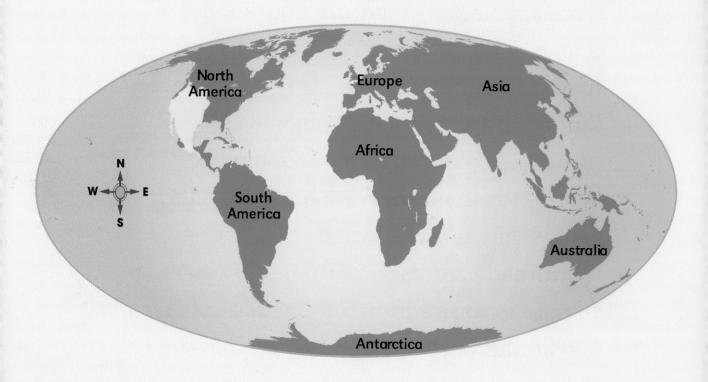

North America

Europe

Asia

Africa

South America

Australia

Antarctica

N
W — E
S

[ ] **Where Horned Lizards Live**

Horned Lizards in the World

Horned lizards live in North America. Eight **species** of horned lizards live in the United States and Canada. Another six species live in Mexico and Guatemala. In the United States, horned lizards live as far east as Arkansas, as far west as California, and as far north as southern South Dakota.

Lizards need warm temperatures. Most lizards live in places where the ground never freezes. Horned lizards can survive colder temperatures by **hibernating** during winter.

Horned Lizard Habitats

Most horned lizards live in deserts, but you can find them in other **habitats**. Some make their homes in prairies and forests. You might even find some horned lizards living on mountains.

All of these habitats have one thing in common—lots of loose sand or soil. Horned lizards like to dig. If they get too hot, they cover themselves up to their heads to escape the heat. They spend their nights buried in the ground.

◀ A horned lizard suns itself on a rock in the Sonoran Desert of Arizona.

What Horned Lizards Eat

Horned lizards eat ants, ants, and more ants. They can eat hundreds of ants each day. If horned lizards can't find ants, they will eat beetles, butterflies, or other small insects.

Horned lizards do not go out of their way to hunt ants. They hang out by the scent trails that ants use to find food. Horned lizards stay still and wait for the ants to pass by. Then they flick out their sticky tongues to snatch the ants. After a few weeks, horned lizards move on to a new trail. If the lizards stay too long, the ants stop using the trails.

◀ A hungry horned lizard uses its sticky tongue to catch ants and other food.

The Life Cycle of a Horned Lizard

Egg*

Hatchling

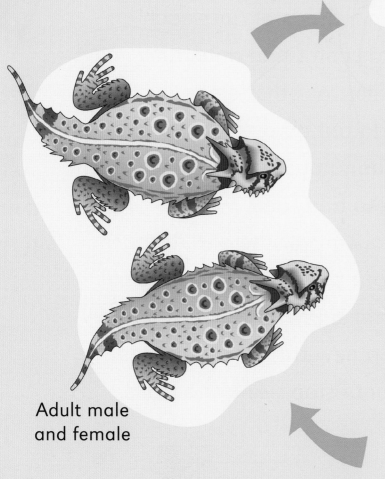

Adult male
and female

2-year-old
horned lizard

*Some horned lizards do not hatch from eggs
outside their mothers' bodies. They hatch
inside, and the mothers give live birth.

14

Producing Young

Horned lizards **mate** in late spring or early summer. After hibernating over winter, horned lizards dig out of the sand. Males begin to look for females.

Female horned lizards carry groups of eggs called **clutches**. Clutches can have two dozen or more eggs.

Some females lay their eggs in the ground. After a few weeks, hatchlings tear through the eggs to get out. Other females carry the eggs inside their bodies until they hatch. Hatchlings are then born alive in thin sacs.

Growing Up

Horned lizard parents don't stick around to raise their young. Hatchlings must find their own food and shelter. They look for places with lots of ants and dig into the ground nearby. Burrowing keeps young horned lizards safe from predators.

Young horned lizards look just like adults, but smaller. They can move and find food as well as adults can. Every few months, young horned lizards outgrow their skin. The top layer dries out and flakes off. The new skin underneath fits their growing bodies.

◀ Horned lizard hatchlings leave their eggs to begin looking for food.

Dangers to Horned Lizards

Spiny horned lizard skin doesn't keep away all predators. Birds, such as shrikes, roadrunners, and hawks, will eat horned lizards they find hidden in the sand. Wolves and coyotes also eat horned lizards.

People don't eat horned lizards, but they are still a big threat. They build cities and homes in deserts, leaving fewer places for horned lizards to live. People also kill ants. Without ants, horned lizards have less food. Some states have laws protecting horned lizards and their habitats.

◄ Roadrunners have tough, expandable throats to allow them to swallow horned lizards.

Amazing Facts about Horned Lizards

- If a horned lizard gets scared enough, it can squirt blood from its eyes.
- Some horned lizards puff up like spiny balloons to scare away predators. Others flatten out like pancakes to hide.
- Horned lizards have to watch out for swarming ants. Red ants swarm to defend their nests. Their venom can kill horned lizards.
- Horned lizards can change their skin colors from lighter to darker to absorb more heat from the sun.

◄ Horned lizards can shoot blood from their eyes as far as 3 feet (1 meter).

Glossary

clutch (KLUHCH)—a group of eggs from a female lizard

cold-blooded (KOHLD-BLUHD-id)—having a body temperature that is the same as the surroundings; all reptiles are cold-blooded.

habitat (HAB-uh-tat)—the place and natural conditions where an animal lives

hibernate (HYE-bur-nate)—to spend winter in a deep sleep

mate (MAYT)—to join together to produce young

predator (PRED-uh-tur)—an animal that hunts other animals for food

species (SPEE-sheez)—a group of plants or animals that share common characteristics; members of the same species can mate and have offspring.

Read More

Claybourne, Anna. *Lizards.* The Secret World Of. Chicago: Raintree, 2004.

Schaefer, Lola M. *Horned Toads.* Heinemann Read and Learn. Tiny-Spiny Animals. Chicago: Heinemann Library, 2004.

Internet Sites

FactHound offers a safe, fun way to find Internet sites related to this book. All of the sites on FactHound have been researched by our staff.

Here's how:
1. Visit *www.facthound.com*
2. Type in this special code **0736854215** for age-appropriate sites. Or enter a search word related to this book for a more general search.
3. Click on the **Fetch It** button.

FactHound will fetch the best sites for you!

Index